· MEET ·
LEONARDO DA VINCI

Read With You Center for
Excellence in STEAM Education

Read With You

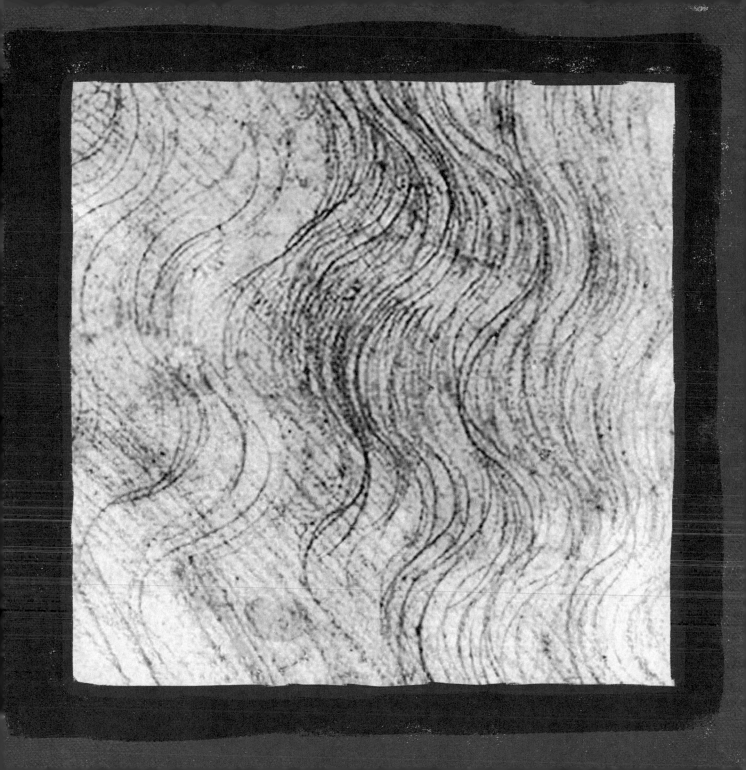

Self Portrait, 1512

Lady with an Ermine, c. 1490

The Annunciation, c. 1472

The Last Supper, c. 1494–1498

The Virgin and Child with Saint Anne, c. 1503–1519

The Portrait of a Musician, c. 1485

Mona Lisa, c. 1503–1519

La Scapigliata, c. 1492–1501

Find Examples

This painting is titled *The Virgin of the Rocks* (c. 1483-1494). It is painted with oil paint, which makes the light colors bright, and the dark colors deep.

How do the light and shadows make the fabric look more real?

Which places are the brightest?

Often, the brightest parts of da Vinci's paintings make the corners of a triangle. Can you find another picture in the story where you can draw a line or shape between some of the people?

Connect

These sketches are *Compositional Sketches for the Virgin Adoring the Christ Child, with and without the Infant, Saint John the Baptist* (c. 1480-1485).

Da Vinci made sketches before he made full paintings. Which of these sketches would make the most beautiful painting?

What colors would you add?

Where would you use dark colors, and where would you use light colors?

Which of your favorite stories do you think would make a beautiful painting?

Craft

Option 1

1. Think of your favorite activity to do outside. Draw an outline of you doing that activity.

2. Fill the background in with as much detail as you can! Draw trees, people, buildings, animals, and more.

3. Fill in your outline of yourself to complete the picture.

Option 2

1. Think of your favorite story. Sketch a scene from that story. Group the people together in a triangular shape.

2. Color it in. Make the dark colors very dark and the light colors very bright to show contrast.

Made in the USA
Las Vegas, NV
19 June 2023